Pieces of my heart

Publisher: BoD – Books on Demand, Stockholm, Sweden
Printer: BoD – Books on Demand, Norderstedt, Germany
ISBN: 978-91-7569-709-3

Can we talk about the fact

that while others see stars

in their lovers' eyes

I see galaxies

in yours?

All I want

is for you to not be

temporary

I know

that I should hate the fact

that I fell for you.

But I don't.

I really don't.

I'd do it all again

without ever looking back.

I fell in love with

looking at you at night,

knowing that you'd still be there

in the morning

Kisses through the window

holding hands with gloves

heads on separate pillows

thoughts fluttering like doves

talking softly on the phone

without knowing what to say

there might as well be oceans

lying in our way

I never needed you

to be my hero.

I just needed the support

to become my own.

I'm your bittersweet coffee

and you're my favourite

cup of tea

I've seen enough grenades

to know that you're

a bomb

I hate all the love quotes

I can't relate to.

They make me feel like

our love was wrong

somehow.

It wasn't your fault.

You never changed.

I just realised that I did.

It's just hard, you know?
Falling for someone
who's in the wrong place
at the wrong time
without knowing
if you'll ever catch up.

I want my kisses

to be the most important thing

that you receive

all day

I don't want to want you

but I still do

I should have known

that you weren't the one

when you said you didn't care for

my favourite song

You and me

were never meant to be

other than in the fantasy

that I created

in my sleep

I tried to take you in
but I never had room
for another broken soul

Fighting doesn't mean I don't love you
and ignoring you
doesn't mean I don't care.
It's just that you're the one
who matters most
and sometimes when you hurt me
I just don't think it's fair.

I know

I broke you.

But I kind of broke

me too.

They say that love is blind

but all I ever wanted

was to see it

with you

The more I think about you
the more I realise
that I don't really miss you
at all anymore.
And somehow
that hurts so much more
than missing you ever could.

You were simply

my band aid

when I was in need

of the whole medical box

A million poets
could not compose
a poem
that would do you
justice

I'd like for you

to keep warm

without having to set me

on fire

I got myself

tangled up in you.

We were joined together

by love

and fear

of loneliness.

You were a part of me

like no one

ever was.

Your lips taste

like my future

It truly amazes me
how little it takes
for you to put
a smile on my face

Our love is but a dot

on the map that is the universe

with all its stars and galaxies

and still

our love means nothing less

than everything to me.

I'm afraid
that I might turn you
into nothing more
than a beautiful mistake

One of us lied

when both of us said

that our love

would last

forever

Your voice feels as soft

as the pillow

underneath my head

I don't know

if you are just a phase,

or something

that has truly changed me

And I genuinely believe
that one day
the world will twist
and turn
and crumble,
and succumb to the perfection
that is you.

All that's left of you

is lipstick

on a wineglass

Your lips against mine
felt so wrong
but yet so right
and your hand
against my thigh
made me hoping
that it wasn't just
a stupid, drunk mistake
this time

I put us out
like a cigarette
leaving you
with nothing
but smoke

How I long

at night

for your lips

in the morning

Your body

is a map

of something new

that I desperately wish

to explore

How do I tell you
that I'm terrified
of you
giving up on me,
since you're the one
who keeps me breathing,
without sounding
too desperate?

One day

my eyes will stop

searching for you

in crowded rooms

There is something
about the way
you look at me
that makes me want to stay yours
forever

Oh darling

you are a flame

far too bright

for this gloomy world

If walls could tell stories

ours would be

their favourite one

All I want

is for you

to fall for me

just as hard

as I fell for you

Keep all of your clothes on
and come into my bed
and try to take off everything
that's hurting you instead

We always
end up fighting
but never
for each other

Before

I simply saw

the rain

but with you

I started seeing

rainbows

I love

your silence.

It feels quiet

but not empty.

You warned me
that your ride
was only heading for
destruction
and all I could say was
"shotgun"

Love is
being far apart
yet somehow
feeling close

He was the boat

that saved me

from the wild

and stormy sea.

And I found myself

deeper in love

than anyone

should ever be.

The higher we got

the harder

we fell.

We hit the ground

like meteorites.

You were the moon
and I was the tide
I was at your mercy
every single time

Love me like

the autumn loves

green leaves

turning red